The Gateway Arch

BUILDING

AMERICA

The Gateway Arch

Craig A. Doherty and Katherine M. Doherty

A BLACKBIRCH PRESS BOOK

WOODBRIDGE, CONNECTICUT

Special Thanks

The authors wish to thank the many librarians who helped them find the research materials for this series—especially Donna Campbell, Barbara Barbieri, Yvonne Thomas, and the librarians at the New Hampshire State Library.

The publisher would like to thank Laura Mills, archivist from the Jefferson National Expansion Memorial, and Bob Moore and Gary Easton of the National Park Service, for their valuable help and cooperation on this project.

Published by Blackbirch Press, Inc.
260 Amity Road
Woodbridge, CT 06525

Email: staff@blackbirch.com
Web Site: www.blackbirch.com

© 1995 Blackbirch Press, Inc.
First Edition

Printed in China

10 9 8 7 6 5 4

Photo Credits

Cover and title page: ©Steve Vidler/Leo de Wys, Inc.
Pages 13, 17, 20, 23, 24, 26–29, 31, 33–36, 39: courtesy Jefferson National Expansion Memorial/National Park Service; page 4: ©Steve Vidler/Leo de Wys, Inc.; page 6: New York Public Library; page 9: National Portrait Gallery; page 14: ©Stan Ries/Leo de Wys, Inc.; page 18: AP/Wide World Photos; page 41: ©Jeff Christensen/Gamma Liaison; pages 42–43: ©Steve Vidler/ Leo de Wys, Inc.

Library of Congress Cataloging-in-Publication Data

Doherty, Katherine M.
   The Gateway Arch / by Katherine M. Doherty and Craig A. Doherty.—1st ed.
      p. cm.—(Building America)
   Includes bibliographical references and index.
   ISBN 1-56711-105-X
   1. Gateway Arch (Saint Louis, Mo.)—History—Juvenile literature. 2. Arches—Missouri— Saint Louis—Design and construction—Juvenile literature. 3. Saint Louis (Mo.)— Buildings, structures, etc.—Juvenile literature. [1. Gateway Arch (Saint Louis, Mo.)— History. 2. Saint Louis (Mo.)—Buildings, structures, etc.] I. Doherty, Craig A. II. Title. III. Series: Building America (Woodbridge, Conn.)
   TA660.A7D64 1995   94-36556
   725'.96—dc20   CIP
                                                                      AC

Table of Contents

Introduction

The Jefferson National Expansion Memorial was created in the 1930s to remind the people of St. Louis, Missouri—and the rest of the world—of the important role that St. Louis played in the westward expansion of our country. Today, the resulting arch (known as the "Gateway Arch") fulfills the vision of the early supporters of the memorial. It also stands as one of the great engineering marvels of the modern era. The 630-foot-high arch is unique, and its polished stainless-steel outer surface can be seen from more than 30 miles away. Designing and building the arch presented engineering challenges that had never before been faced. Like the brave pioneers who passed through St. Louis on their way into the unknown lands to the west, the people who built the arch succeeded in meeting and overcoming all the obstacles that were laid before them.

Opposite: When the sun shines upon it, the stainless-steel "Gateway Arch" can be seen from more than 30 miles away.

The First Challenges

In the 19th century, St. Louis, Missouri, was one of the major cities on the Mississippi River. It was the starting point for countless westbound explorers, trappers, and settlers. By the 1930s, however, the city had lost much of its vibrancy. Traffic on the river had all but stopped, and the United States was well settled from coast to coast. Warehouses that had rented for $20,000 to $30,000 a year in the mid-19th century stood empty; and those with tenants were renting for $1,000 a year. The riverfront, which had

Opposite:
St. Louis in 1841. Located near where the Missouri River meets the mighty Mississippi, the city has always been heavily trafficked by traders, trappers, and westbound explorers.

7

Thomas Jefferson and the Louisiana Purchase

Thomas Jefferson

Thomas Jefferson, an important participant in the creation of the United States, was the nation's third president (1801-1809). As a man, he embodied the spirit of the country he helped to create. He was trained as a lawyer and became one of the leading statesmen of his age. In addition, he was a self-trained architect, a plantation owner, and the principal writer of America's Declaration of Independence. Despite all his talents and contributions, Jefferson asked that only three of his accomplishments appear on his tombstone: "author of the Declaration of Independence, of the Statute of Virginia for religious freedom, and the father of the University of Virginia."

been the heart of St. Louis, was empty and, for the most part, dead.

When Luther Ely Smith, a St. Louis lawyer, finally visited Vincennes, Indiana, in 1933, he was pleased by the George Rogers Clark Memorial that had been constructed there, partly through his efforts. Smith then thought that St. Louis should have its own memorial as well—one that paid tribute to the westward expansion of the country. He shared his idea with St. Louis's mayor, Bernard F. Dickmann.

Although it was not included on his tombstone, one of the most important acts associated with Thomas Jefferson was the purchase from France of 800,000 square miles of territory west of the Mississippi River. As president, Jefferson sent James Monroe and Robert Livingston to France in 1803, in an effort to secure a treaty that allowed the free use of the Mississippi River by people from the United States. Jefferson soon received word that Napoleon Bonaparte, the leader of France, was willing to sell to the United States all the French land west of the Mississippi River for the attractive price of $15 million. Napoleon was involved in a war with Haiti and his army had just suffered enormous losses. Because of the difficulties and defeats his army faced, Napoleon had a much greater need for the $15 million than he did for the land in North America.

Jefferson had some reservations about the purchase. Among them was his feeling that the U.S. Constitution had no provisions allowing the federal government to acquire new lands. Despite his constitutional concerns, he easily won congressional approval and went ahead with the treaty and the purchase. On December 20, 1803, in a ceremony in New Orleans, the French turned over the lands known as the Louisiana Territory to the United States. With the new territory added, the size of the country nearly doubled.

In 1804, Jefferson sent out an expedition, led by Meriwether Lewis and William Clark, to explore the newly acquired lands. The detailed reports sent back by the Lewis and Clark Expedition's two-year trip greatly excited the country while Jefferson was into his second term as president.

Enthusiastic about such a memorial, Mayor Dickmann called a number of prominent St. Louis residents together for a meeting in December 1933. The people who attended the meeting formed the Jefferson National Expansion Memorial Association in 1934, and Luther Ely Smith was elected the chairman of the group.

Events progressed rapidly at first. The state of Missouri granted the organization a charter, and the idea for a memorial was forwarded to Washington, D.C. There, it was hoped that federal approval and matching funds would be forthcoming. The U.S. Congress quickly passed a bill that set up the U.S. Territorial Expansion Memorial Commission and provided for matching funding to acquire the land. The bill was signed into law by President Franklin D. Roosevelt on June 19, 1934. It seemed that St. Louis would soon have a memorial not only to President Thomas Jefferson, but also to all the other people involved in the expansion and settlement of America during the 1800s.

Problems, Delays, and More Problems

With congressional and presidential approval of the plan in place, no one involved with the memorial at the time would have believed it would take an additional 30 years to complete the project.

In 1935, the people of St. Louis voted $2.25 million in bonds to pay for their share of the acquisition of the site. (To finance large public projects, local government money is often used to back a loan from a bank. To secure the loan, bonds—public money— are issued as repayment promises. The issuing of bonds must be approved by the voters of the city or community.) President Roosevelt signed an executive order designating the area as part of the national park system. This authorized the expenditure of $6.75 million in federal matching funds, and directed the U.S. secretary of the interior to acquire the land for the memorial. The site and the project then became the responsibility of the National Park Service, and by June 1939, it had acquired almost all of the land needed. Demolition of the old warehouses along the river began on October 10, 1939. Within three years, the entire 37-block area had been leveled.

Close to the site of the memorial stands a building called the Old Courthouse, which was built between 1839 and 1862. It is a building of great historical significance because several important cases were tried there. Most famous among these was the trial that resulted in the 1857 Dred Scott Decision (a U.S. Supreme Court case that said the government could place no regulations on where slavery could exist). By 1940, the city of St. Louis was going to let the Old Courthouse simply deteriorate until it could be torn down. However, Charles E. Peterson and John Albury Bryan—who had been collecting artifacts from the buildings that were demolished—fought to save the historic site. They were successful, and, in 1940, President Roosevelt approved the transfer of ownership from the city of St. Louis to the Park Service. The Old Courthouse is now part of the Jefferson National Expansion Memorial and houses a number of historical exhibits.

By 1942, the entire Jefferson Memorial project had been put on hold. During this time, the area was used as a parking lot. America had entered World War II just a year earlier and could not afford to use any resources on projects not related to the war effort. When World War II ended in 1945, the country's concerns were quickly turned to other problems. The St. Louis memorial, however, was not one of them. Nevertheless, the people involved in the Memorial Association attempted to move forward on their own. Those planning the memorial had considered a variety of design ideas between 1933 and 1947. One design that had been proposed included a

THE GATEWAY CITY

The arch dominates the downtown skyline of St. Louis.

large statue of Jefferson with obelisks (tall, tapering structures) and three museums. Another envisioned seven groups of statues and a number of buildings.

When members of the Memorial Association had first met in 1933 and 1934, they discussed holding a

St. Louis is the largest city in Missouri. Located at the eastern edge of the state, on the Mississippi, it was founded by a French fur trader, Pierre Laclede, who named the settlement after the patron saint of France. St. Louis remained a relatively quiet trading post until 1803, when it became part of the United States with the Louisiana Purchase. After Lewis and Clark returned from their exploration of the area, settlers began to arrive in St. Louis. Many others also passed through on their way west. As the traffic north and south on the Mississippi River grew, and the westward movement of settlers increased, so did the size of the city. In 1818, Saint Louis University became the first college west of the Mississippi. A major newspaper of the city, the *St. Louis Dispatch*, was founded by Joseph Pulitzer, for whom the famous Pulitzer Prize is named.

By the late 1800s, St. Louis had become a major railroad center, second only to Chicago in rail traffic. Today, it is still the nation's busiest inland river port and a prosperous city with great diversity of industry. The riverfront has been revitalized by the Jefferson National Expansion Memorial, and its effect on the city has been far-reaching.

The positive impact of the arch on the city also includes an increase in civic pride, boosted tourism, and renovation of the area surrounding the arch. Many of the old warehouses in the area, similar to the ones torn down to build the arch, have been converted into thriving offices, studios, shops, and restaurants. In the time since the Gateway Arch first opened, more than 2,000 hotel rooms have been built in St. Louis. The influx of tourists to the city has created a number of jobs and has added a new dimension to the local economy.

Since the first person rode the tramway to the top of the arch in 1967, more than 65 million people have visited the memorial. About 2.7 million of those visitors came in 1993 alone. On a busy summer day, as many as 30,000 people will visit the arch, and 5,500 of them will ride the tramway to the top.

national design contest for the memorial. In 1947, they decided to return to this plan, and raised $225,000 to fund the competition. The association offered $75,000 in prize money and received 172 entries from architects and designers from around the country.

Designing the Arch

The criteria for the 1947 design competition were set by the Memorial Association. Each design submitted had to include five basic features: an architectural memorial, a museum dedicated to old St. Louis, a living memorial to Thomas Jefferson, a plan for recreational use of the memorial site, and provisions for moving the site's historic railroad tracks. Plans for building the anticipated nearby interstate highway were also requested.

Opposite:
Eero Saarinen's modern design is based on a catenary arch and was inspired by Roman architecture.

15

Of the 172 entries in the design competition, 5 were chosen as finalists after four days of discussions by a panel of nationally respected architects. Then the five designs were critiqued by the panel, by members of the National Park Service, and by the Memorial Association. After that round of discussion, each finalist was asked to submit a revised, detailed design. On February 17, 1948, the arch design of now-famous architect Eero Saarinen was chosen by unanimous vote on the first ballot. A group of architecture students from the University of Illinois came in second and won $30,000.

A Catenary Arch

Saarinen's winning design was unique among the competitors. One person commented that, "so many of the other designs for this memorial were merely spinoffs of other memorials . . . nothing came close to the arch." Saarinen felt that simple shapes like the pyramids and obelisks of ancient Egypt make the best memorials because, in their simplicity, they have maintained their significance and dignity throughout the ages.

Eero Saarinen saw the memorial as symbolizing a gateway. He therefore decided that something that recalled the triumphal arches of the ancient Romans would be appropriate. But he also wanted his arch to be on the cutting edge of modern design. For this reason, he chose an inverted "catenary" arch for the memorial.

A catenary curve is the curve that a chain makes when it is suspended loosely between two points. Not only would this shape give Saarinen the simple

Opposite:
Architect Eero Saarinen crouches with a few scale models of his winning design.

MASTER ARCHITECT

Eero Saarinen

Eero Saarinen once said, "Architecture should, among other things, fulfill man's belief in the nobility of his existence." The Gateway Arch stands today as a fulfillment of this belief.

Eero Saarinen was born in 1910, in Finland. There, his father, Eliel, was an architect and his mother, Loja, was a sculptor and artisan. As a young boy, Eero had already started to follow in his father's footsteps. At age 12, he

elegance he wanted, it would also retain the architectural strength needed for such a large-scale design. Once he decided on the catenary arch, he had to figure out how to build it. His final design created an arch whose base at each end is an equilateral triangle with 54-foot sides. As the arch curves upward from the bases, it tapers, so that, at the top of the arch, its cross section is an equilateral triangle with 17-foot sides.

The arch utilized the most modern construction techniques that were available at the time. Rather

won a matchstick design contest. When he was 13, his family moved to Michigan, where his father founded the famous Cranbrook Institute of Architecture and Design.

Saarinen studied at the Yale School of Architecture from 1930 to 1934, and then spent two years studying in Europe. In 1936, he returned to Cranbrook and became a partner in his father's architectural firm. Over the next few years, he taught design at the institute and assisted his father on a number of important jobs.

In 1947, at the age of 37, Saarinen entered the Jefferson National Expansion Memorial design contest on his own. It became his first major success. After winning the memorial competition, Saarinen went on to design a number of notable projects, including the General Motors Technical Center near Detroit, the Trans World Airlines terminal at Kennedy International Airport in New York, and Dulles International Airport near Washington, D.C.

Saarinen never got to see the completed Gateway Arch, which some consider his greatest design. He died of a brain tumor in 1961, the same year that the ground-breaking ceremony was held for his brilliant structure in St. Louis.

than building a frame and covering it with a steel skin, the stainless-steel outer layer was designed to be the actual supporting frame of the structure. This is called an "orthotropic" design. Because of the radical departure from traditional design, new building methods were initiated to construct the arch. There was some concern about the strength of the frame and what would happen to it in high winds. Wind-tunnel tests, done in 1948, proved that it would take winds of more than 150 miles an hour to harm the structure.

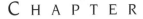
Building the Arch

After the Korean War (1950-1953), the people of the United States experienced a time of relative peace and prosperity, and attention in St. Louis once again turned toward building the so-called Gateway Arch. Before the project could get back underway, however, problems with the railroad tracks had to be resolved.

Opposite:
Here, about
60 feet below
ground level,
workers prepare
a section of what
would later be
the underground
visitor center.

Working on the Railroad

In the 1880s, a double set of raised tracks had been built through the area, and they needed to somehow be relocated if the arch was to be built. The issue of moving the tracks caused much controversy among officials of the city, the railroads, and various government agencies. Eugene Mackey, head of the St. Louis chapter of the American Institute of Architects, conducted a survey that helped clarify the problems involved. He presented his findings to the mayor of St. Louis, Raymond R. Tucker. Mayor Tucker, who had been an engineer, came up with a compromise solution in 1957.

Tucker's solution called for a location change for both the arch and the tracks: The tracks would be moved a few feet farther away from the river and sunk below the level of the arch. At one point, the tracks would run underground, giving the arch site direct access to the river. The arch, in Tucker's solution, would be moved to higher ground.

Design Changes

Mayor Tucker's compromise forced Eero Saarinen to rethink his design, which had originally included a sculpture arcade, museums, restaurants, a historic village, a campfire theater, and other recreational features. The redesigned memorial would still be dominated by the same catenary arch, but most of the other aspects of the design were replaced with an underground visitor center that would lie between the two legs of the arch.

As is often the case with a compromise, not everyone was happy. With this new plan, the Lisa Warehouse, a historic building that was renovated to serve as a historic structure, had to be torn down. During demolition of the area, John Albury Bryan, a St. Louis architect, had collected architectural artifacts for a proposed museum of architecture. Most of these artifacts were eventually either given away or destroyed. Only a small quantity of the artifacts were preserved and stored. Many people, however, found the cleaner, starker setting for the arch even more interesting and appealing than that of the previous plan.

On September 6, 1958, President Dwight D. Eisenhower signed a law that gave $17.25 million in matching funds for the construction of the memorial. On June 23, 1959, a ground-breaking ceremony was held to signal the start of the track-relocation project. The MacDonald Construction Company of St. Louis was awarded the contract to relocate the tracks. It would later receive the contracts for the arch and the shell of the visitor center as well.

Building a Solid Foundation

The way it is designed, the arch seems to just spring out of the earth. The foundations on which it sits,

Before construction on the actual foundations could begin, workers had to blast away 30 feet of top soil and 30 feet of rock.

In June 1962, almost 26,000 tons of concrete were poured to create the arch's two foundations. By October, as shown here, the supporting structures were nearly complete.

however, were carefully engineered and extend far below the surface. Some 300,000 cubic feet of material had to be removed to build the foundations. After removing 30 feet of soil, the workers blasted away 30 feet of rock so that the arch would be anchored to solid bedrock.

Starting on June 27, 1962, construction workers poured almost 26,000 tons of concrete into two 60-foot-deep holes. The engineers were concerned about the stresses that would be placed on the concrete footings, so they devised a unique way of

LABOR AND CIVIL RIGHTS

Most of the workers on the Jefferson National Expansion Memorial found the job interesting and challenging. The ethnic makeup of the workers, however, did create some controversy. The arch was built during a time of growing awareness about racial discrimination in America. It was also a time when people became more active in standing up for their rights.

One July morning in 1964, civil rights activists Percy Green and Richard Daly climbed up on the legs of the arch and demanded that African Americans from unions be hired to work on the memorial. Today, thanks in part to people like Green and Daly, there are laws that prohibit companies from discriminating against people for such unjust reasons as race, sex, and age.

"pre-stressing" the concrete to strengthen it and keep it from cracking. A total of 252 steel-tensioning bars were set 34 feet deep into the concrete. As each layer of concrete was setting, workers would move from steel bar to steel bar—in a sequence predetermined by the engineers—and attach a hydraulic jack to the bar. The jack would exert 71 tons of pressure on the drying concrete. This compressed the material and made it stronger.

Pre-stressing was considered a dangerous process because of the great force being applied to the concrete and the individual steel bars. Every precaution was taken to prevent injuries if one of the steel bars snapped under the pressure of the jack. Fortunately, none of the bars broke, and the pre-stressing of the concrete was completed without mishap.

From Steel to Shining Steel

On February 12, 1963, two years after the death of Eero Saarinen, the first stainless-steel section was placed on the south leg of the arch. The first section

Workers set up scaffolding against the first steel sections of the arch in March 1963.

had a 54-foot-sided equilateral triangle base, was 12 feet high, and weighed more than 50 tons. The steel sections of the arch were built in Pennsylvania by the Pittsburgh-Des Moines Steel Company and were shipped to St. Louis by rail. Each steel section had an outer skin of 1/4-inch-thick stainless steel and an inner skin of 3/8-inch-thick carbon steel. In the first sections, the two skins were 35 inches apart, while at the top they tapered to only 7 5/8 inches apart.

When the sections arrived, they had to be welded together by the workers at the site. A special flatbed railroad car was built to move the welded sections from the assembly area to the base of the

The first six stainless-steel sections were in place by June 1963.

arch. There, each section was lifted by a crane into position. The crane held the triangular-shaped section in place, while the workers bolted it and welded it to the section below. For the first 300 feet of each leg, the space between the inner and outer skin was filled with concrete, which strengthened the entire structure.

A special rig on tracks, called a creeper derrick, was devised to carry the cranes into the air as the arch was built.

The first six sections of each leg were lifted into place by conventional cranes. After the legs of the arch were 72 feet high, however, the engineers had to devise another way to lift the sections into place. Special rigs, called "creeper derricks," were designed to climb the legs of the arch.

On each leg of the arch there was one creeper derrick. This consisted of a set of tracks bolted to the outside of the arch, and a tiltable 43-foot by 32-foot crane platform that could climb the tracks as the arch got taller. Placed on the platform was a 130-foot-tall crane. The entire crane assembly weighed 80 tons. A ladder and an elevator followed the tracks up the arch to the work level.

Working on the arch was both frightening and exciting for the people involved. Several workers had to quit the project because they found it too disorienting to be working on a construction job where nothing was level and none of the corners were square. Other workers found the arch itself so interesting that they were thankful to be a part of the project. Even when the summer temperatures reached 150 degrees Farenheit inside the arch, and when the frigid winds of winter made it almost impossible to keep their welding torches lit, these workers enjoyed their jobs.

Safety was a major issue during construction. All workers wore hard hats, and safety harnesses were worn when necessary. Safety nets were suspended below the workers wherever there was a chance of someone falling a great distance. The special attention to safety paid off; no workers were ever seriously injured on the job.

Tramway to the Top

As the crews continued to work on putting together the sections and setting them in place, other workers were busy inside the arch. Saarinen had designed the structure so that visitors would be able to travel to the top, where there are 16 observation windows on each side. A stairway was built inside the arch,

and utility lines were put in place. The biggest job inside the structure was building the tramways that would transport visitors up to the top.

The tramways had created a number of interesting design and engineering problems to

A *head-on view of the arch during construction shows how it was created from a series of triangles.*

be overcome. Because of the changing angles of the arch, a conventional elevator or escalator could not be used. The design also had to work around the fact that the inside of the span had 48-foot sides at the base of the legs but only 15.5-foot sides at the top. Finally, an elevator expert named Dick Bowser came up with a solution. He designed a tram with free-swinging compartments for the passengers, similar to the seats on a Ferris wheel. Each of the two trams, one in each leg of the arch, had eight compartments that each sat five people. Today, on an average busy summer day, more than 5,500 people ride this unique tram to the top.

Bridging the Gap

As the two legs of the arch climbed skyward, the engineers kept a careful eye on their progress. During the day, the sides of the arch would expand and contract depending on the position and the intensity of the sun at any given time. Therefore, the engineers had to make all their detailed measurements at night when the entire arch was the same temperature. Keeping the two legs perfectly aligned was critical if they were going to meet at the top as planned. If the measurements were off by as little as 1/64 of an inch at the base, the legs would not meet at the top.

One thing the engineers had to worry about was the possibility that the weight of the derricks and other construction equipment might bend the legs of the arch. To prevent this, they installed a stabilizing strut at the 530-foot level. The strut weighed 60 tons and supported the two legs while the last 21 sections were added to each leg. By September 1965,

the creeper derricks had reached the height of 595 feet and could go no further. The last 35 feet of the arch could be reached only with their long booms.

On October 28, 1965, only one eight-foot section was needed to complete the arch. Before it could be put in place, however, the legs on either side needed to be pried apart. The two 8,000-ton legs had leaned in so that they were only 2.5 feet apart at the top, even with the stabilizing strut in place.

The arch's giant stabilizing strut sits on the ground before being raised about 500 feet in the air.

By September 1965, only a few final sections were needed to connect the two legs of the arch.

Spreader jacks were used to push the two legs far enough apart to insert the last section. As the workers put this last piece in, fire trucks sprayed water on the lower parts of the south leg to keep it from expanding in the sunlight. When the jacks were

released, 325 tons of force exerted by the two legs clamped the last section in place while it was bolted and welded. As the assembly of the exterior of the arch was completed, the large crowd that watched from the ground cheered. Many others in the area watched the momentous event on television.

The final section of the arch is hoisted into place high above the city of St. Louis.

Finishing Touches

Although the arch was complete, there was still a great deal of work to do on the underground visitor center, on the grounds, and inside the arch. On October 19, 1965, the federal government added another $5 million to their matching funds to insure that the project would be completed.

It was now time for the creeper derricks to slowly descend the 595 feet back down to the ground. As

Opposite:
An aerial view of the arch, soon after major construction was completed in October 1965.

37

the derricks moved down, the tracks above them were unbolted from the arch and lowered as well. Workers filled the bolt holes, and the entire stainless-steel outer skin of the arch was cleaned.

Inside the arch and underground, work continued on the transit system and the visitor center. On June 3, 1967, the Museum of Westward Expansion opened in temporary quarters in the visitor center. On July 24, 1967, the first passengers rode the north leg tram to the top of the arch. The south tram was finished on March 19, 1968, and the north tram was shut down for two months to do some finishing work in the loading area.

Dedication and Beyond

When the arch and the visitor center were officially dedicated on May 25, 1968, Vice-President Hubert Humphrey gave the dedication speech, and Secretary of the Interior Stewart L. Udall was the master of ceremonies. Although the arch itself was officially completed, there was still a lot of work to be done on the grounds and on other components of the memorial.

A number of people felt that the arch should be illuminated at night, and the National Park Service studied the idea in 1966 and 1967. Five companies were asked to submit plans to light the arch, but the problems created by its size and its reflective surface made lighting the arch impractical. This was also a time when the government was becoming aware of the need to save energy. The Park Service had been instructed to reduce energy use by 14 percent, and lighting the arch would have only increased energy

use. To this day, the sun, moon, stars, and lights of the city of St. Louis are the arch's only sources of illumination.

Upon completion of the main structure, the grounds of the memorial still needed substantial work. Saarinen's design had called for a Grand Staircase, consisting of 64 steps, leading from the

Finishing work followed the placement of the arch's final section. Here, during November 1965, welders put final touches on the top of the structure.

THE RIVER RISES IN 1993

An aerial view shows the Grand Staircase and many of the steps completely under water after the flooding of 1993.

arch site down to Wharf Street, which runs along the bank of the Mississippi River. There were also two overlooks in the original site plans, so that visitors to the memorial would be able to see the river from ground level. The Grand Staircase was completed and dedicated on June 24, 1976, and the overlooks were completed soon after.

The Museum of Westward Expansion had not been part of Saarinen's original plan, but it had been added at the request of the Park Service in 1960. When the visitor center was excavated, a 150-foot by 290-foot cavern was created with a dirt floor and a concrete ceiling supported by 40 columns. The cavern sat for ten years waiting for funds to build

The Mississippi River, which passes by St. Louis on its 2,348-mile journey to the Gulf of Mexico, drains approximately forty percent (or 1.25 million square miles) of the United States. Its largest tributary is America's longest river, the Missouri, which enters the Mississippi near St. Louis. During the spring and summer of 1993, the Missouri and Mississippi river drainages received record-breaking rainfall—more than 30 inches between April 1 and July 26—as one weather system after another stalled over the Midwest.

In many places, the rivers rose over their levees, which are small dams designed to prevent flooding on lowlands. Entire towns and millions of acres of farmland were flooded. In St. Louis, the arch became the focal point of many flood watchers. Fortunately, the French who settled St. Louis had wisely put the city above the river on a series of natural bluffs, or hills, and the arch sits atop one of those bluffs.

During the floods, the arch remained open, even though water was seeping into the lower levels of the visitor center. Pumps were used to remove more than 1,000 gallons per minute from the inside. The boulevard at the base of the Grand Staircase was under water, and the level of the river reached almost halfway up the 64 steps. In August, the waters finally began to recede. Many victims of the floods took inspiration from the arch and the courage it represents while repairing their homes and rebuilding their lives.

the permanent home for the museum. The museum, which eventually cost more than $3.1 million to complete, opened on August 10, 1976, with the biggest celebration the arch had ever seen.

One month earlier, on July 4, 1976—the bicentennial of the Declaration of Independence—800,000 people had crowded the national memorial and the surrounding area to celebrate the 200th birthday of the United States. For many, it was also a celebration of the Jefferson National Expansion Memorial and Eero Saarinen's brilliant design. Together, they have revitalized the city of St. Louis and stand forever as a reminder of the millions of brave and rugged individuals that have taken a part in the building of America.

The grace and elegance of the arch's simple outline make it one of the most unique and striking structures ever built.

GLOSSARY

arch A curved geometric shape.

bedrock The solid rock that is under the earth's surface.

concrete A mixture of sand, aggregate, cement, and water used as building material and as a surfacing material in walkways and roadways.

creeper derrick A special piece of construction equipment, consisting of a set of tracks on the outside of a structure, a tiltable platform, and a tall crane. Creeper derricks raised the sections of the Gateway Arch so that they could be bolted and welded into place.

engineer A person who is trained in dealing with a variety of construction processes. The arch used civil, mechanical, and structural engineers to assist in the design and construction of the memorial.

equilateral triangle A triangle with three equal sides.

foundation The underlying and supporting base of a structure.

hydraulic jack A device that uses a water-powered pump to lift or apply pressure to something.

inverted catenary arch The "upside-down" version of the curve created when a length of chain is suspended between two points.

obelisk A tall, tapering structure devised by the ancient Egyptians and built from a single piece of stone. A true obelisk tapers to a pyramidal top and is ten times as high as its base is wide.

orthotropic A structural engineering term that means that the skin of a structure actually supports the structure, rather than just covers an inner supporting skeleton. The Gateway Arch is built on the orthotropic principle.

pre-stressing A dangerous process in which stress is applied to concrete while it is setting so that it will be stronger and less likely to crack.

spreader jack A device used to spread and hold open two structural components.

stabilizing strut A structural piece used to support a main structure and to resist pressure upon the structure.

tram A car people stand in or sit in when they are transported by a tramway.

tramway A system of cables and/or tracks that are used to transport people in enclosed cars.

transit system A system that carries people from one point to another.

CHRONOLOGY

1803 Purchase of Louisiana Territory from France doubles the size of the United States.

1933 December 15 Committee is formed to establish a memorial to westward expansion.

1934 April 11 Jefferson National Expansion Memorial Association is established.

1935 December 21 President Franklin D. Roosevelt signs an executive order committing federal support to the acquisition and development of a site for the memorial.

1936 June 22 National Park Service opens an office in St. Louis from which it can oversee the creation of the memorial.

1937 June 3 Process of acquiring the land for the memorial begins.

1939 - 1942 Demolition of buildings in the 37-block area where the memorial is to be built takes place.

1940 May President Roosevelt approves acceptance of the Old Courthouse as part of the Jefferson National Expansion Memorial.

1945 - 1947 Memorial Association raises money to fund design competition.

1947 Memorial Association announces design competition and receives 172 entries.

September 26 Memorial Association announces five finalists.

1948 February 17 Eero Saarinen's arch design is unanimously selected as the winning design for the memorial.

May 25 U.S. Territorial Expansion Memorial Commission approves Saarinen's winning design.

1957 Problems over railroad tracks resolved and Saarinen has to accommodate new location of tracks in his plan.

1958 September 6 President Dwight D. Eisenhower signs Public Law 85-936, authorizing and funding the Jefferson National Expansion Memorial project.

1959 June 18 Railroad Relocation Project is awarded to MacDonald Construction Company of St. Louis.

June 23 Ground-breaking ceremonies take place.

1961 February Excavation for the visitor center and arch foundations begins.

1962 March 14 MacDonald Construction is awarded the contract to build the arch and the visitor center shell.

June 27 First concrete is poured into the deep foundations of the arch.

1963 February 12 First section of the stainless-steel arch is attached to the foundation.

1965 October 28 Last eight-foot stainless-steel section is bolted and welded to the arch; a ceremony is held to mark its completion.

1967 July 14 North leg tramway is opened to the public.

1968 March 18 South leg tramway is opened to the public.

May 25 Vice-President Hubert Humphrey and Secretary of the Interior Stewart L. Udall officiate at the dedication of the memorial.

1976 June 24 Grand Staircase from Wharf Street to the arch is completed and opened.

July 4 About 800,000 people gather at the arch to celebrate the bicentennial of the Declaration of Independence and the founding of the United States.

August 23 Museum of Westward Expansion is dedicated.

1993 Floodwaters threaten but do not close the memorial.

Further Reading

Ayer, Eleanor. *Our National Monuments.* Brookfield, CT: Millbrook Press, 1992.

Boring, Mel. *Incredible Constructions and the People Who Built Them.* New York: Walker & Co., 1985.

Chase, John. *Louisiana Purchase: An American Story.* Gretna, LA: Pelican, 1991.

Crisman, Ruth. *Thomas Jefferson, Man with a Vision.* New York: Scholastic, 1992.

Ford, Barbara. *St. Louis.* New York: Dillon, 1989.

Lambert, Mark. *Building Technology.* Chicago: Watts, 1991.

Morgan, Sally and Morgan, Adrian. *Structures.* New York: Facts On File, 1993.

Nardo, Don. *Thomas Jefferson.* San Diego: Lucent, 1993.

SOURCE NOTES

Archibald, John J. "It's the Top." *St. Louis Post-Dispatch*, July 24, 1987, F-1.

Artega, Robert F. *Building the Arch*. St. Louis: Jefferson National Expansion Historical Association, 1967.

Blake, Peter. "Monument to the Dream." *Interior Design*, v 62, no 1, January 1991, 138-139.

Bryan, Bill. "Free for all Marks Arch's 20th Year." *St. Louis Post-Dispatch*, October 28, 1985, A-3.

Capps, Michael A. "A History of the Gateway Arch." Pamphlet. National Park Service, 1994, 5 pages.

"Competition: Jefferson National Expansion Memorial." *Progressive Architecture*, May 1948, 51-2.

Corbett, Marjorie. "In Pursuit of Civil Rights." *National Parks*, March-April 1987, 20-21.

Corrigan, Patricia. "The Triumph of the Arch." *St. Louis Post-Dispatch*, October 27, 1985.

Ebenhoh, Tom, and Givens, Steve. *Arch Celebration: Commemorating the 25th Anniversary of the Gateway Arch, 1965-1990*. House Springs, MO: Spiritgraphics.

"Engineering of Saarinen's Arch." *Architectural Record*, v 133, May 1963, 188-191.

Gateway Today: Jefferson National Expansion Memorial. St. Louis, 1994.

Graebner, William. "Gateway to Empire: An Interpretation of Eero Saarinen's 1948 Design for St. Louis Arch." *Prospects*, v 18, annual, 1993, 367-399.

"Incredible Gateway Arch." *Popular Mechanics*, v 120, December 1963, 86-90.

"Jefferson Memorial Competition Winners." *Architectural Record*, v 103, April 1948, 92-95.

"Leaping Time and Space." *Time*, v 86, November 19, 1965, 94-5.

McCue, George. "The Arch: An Appreciation." *AIA Journal*, v 67, 1978, 57-63.

"Saarinen, Eero." *Current Biography*, 1949, 541-2.

Singer, Dale. "The Building of Arch Helped St. Louis to Soar." *St. Louis Post-Dispatch*, October 27, 1985.

Spade, Rupert, and Futagawa, Yukio. *Eero Saarinen*. New York: Simon & Schuster, 1971.

"Towering Arch on the River Front." *American City*, v 78, May 1963, 48.

Varga, Tamas. *The Mathematics of the Arch*. University City, MO: Southern Illinois University of Edwardsville, Teachers' Center Project, 1981.

Wood, Sue Ann. "In St. Louis: Why Arch Isn't Lighted." *Chicago Tribune*, October 4, 1992, sec 12, 5.

Zakarian, John J. "Arch of Triumph, U.S. Style." *New York Times*, December 24, 1972, travel section, 4, 7.

INDEX